ISBNs:
978-0-578-34798-1 (paperback)
978-0-578-34955-8 (hardcover)

Published by JT Taylor, LLC

Dedications

To the youth who experience bullying, you are not alone. There's an army of "Bully Exterminators" in your corner.

To Javin, Kyrell, Jenetha, my parents, and brothers for always being in my corner. Your support gives me the motivation to keep pressing forward.

The late Coach Bobbie Stanley, you embodied the characteristics of "Billy the Bully Exterminator", by building confidence in all the student-athletes you coached and mentored.

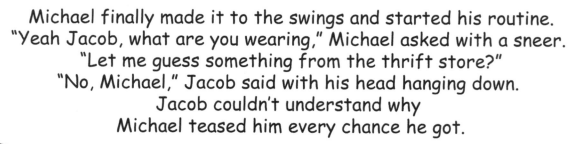

Michael finally made it to the swings and started his routine.
"Yeah Jacob, what are you wearing," Michael asked with a sneer.
"Let me guess something from the thrift store?"
"No, Michael," Jacob said with his head hanging down.
Jacob couldn't understand why
Michael teased him every chance he got.

Bobbie couldn't understand why someone would want to hurt Jacob's feelings.
Later that day, Jacob went to Bobbie's house to work on a school project.
Jacob didn't mention anything about what Michael had said to him.
Bobbie was really confused but didn't say anything about it either.
He didn't want to make Michael feel even more uncomfortable.

The next day at school Bobbie,
Jacob and Michael were together again for gym class.
When it was time to go outside,
Michael tripped Jacob, making him fall. "Are you ok, Jacob?"
Bobbie asked, reaching down to help up his friend.
The gym teacher , Coach McCabe,
gave Jacob some ice to put on his head to stop the swelling.

But Bobbie had been taught differently.
He wanted to change the world – one person at a time
and knew a good way to start was to eliminate bullying.
This way, his friend Jacob would never have to deal with a bully, like Michael, again.
Bobbie also wanted to make sure his friends knew that they could talk to an adult
if someone was bullying them, just like he talked to the adults in his family.

"I'm here to make sure you don't bully any more people," he said.
"Even my friend, Jacob." Michael had no clue that Billy was actually Bobbie.

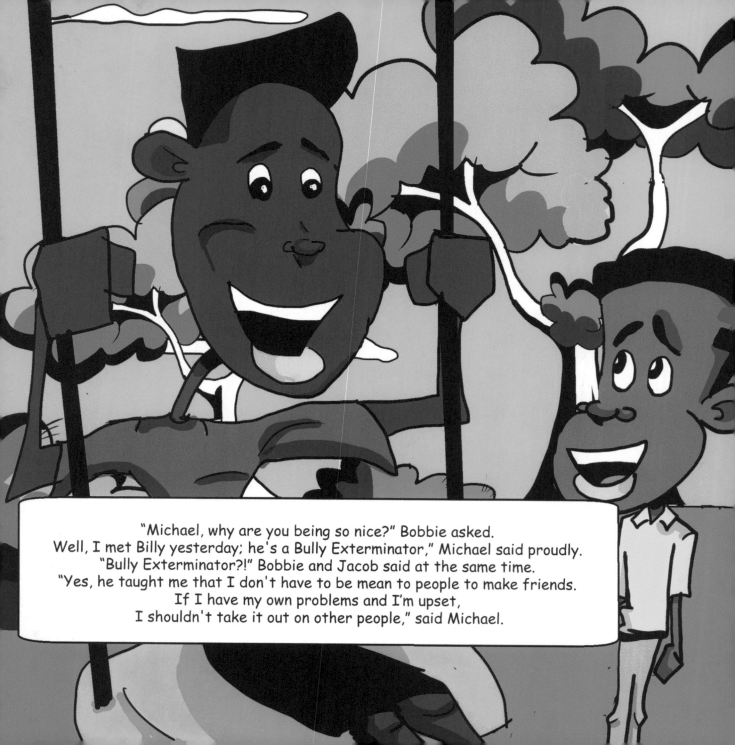

"Michael, why are you being so nice?" Bobbie asked.
Well, I met Billy yesterday; he's a Bully Exterminator," Michael said proudly.
"Bully Exterminator?!" Bobbie and Jacob said at the same time.
"Yes, he taught me that I don't have to be mean to people to make friends.
If I have my own problems and I'm upset,
I shouldn't take it out on other people," said Michael.

"The most important lesson that Billy taught me was,
I don't have to deal with my problems all by myself,"
Michael said, also sounding relieved.
"I can talk to other people that I trust, so I don't feel alone."
Michael was dealing with so many things in his life
that the only way he knew how to ignore them was to bully other people.

And just like that... Billy the Bully Exterminator
had his next mission – enlist everyone that he can to help eliminate bullying.
He was on his way to making sure everyone was treated with kindness
and respect and changing the world – one person at a time.

CPSIA information can be obtained
at www.ICGtesting.com
Printed in the USA
BVHW022034080222
628392BV00002B/78

* 9 7 8 0 5 7 8 3 4 7 9 8 1 *